Exploring History through Simple Recipes

Cooking on Nineteenth-Century Whaling Ships

by Charla L. Draper

Consultant: Judy Downey, Librarian
New Bedford Whaling Museum, New Bedford, Massachusetts

Blue Earth Books

an imprint of Capstone Press
Mankato, Minnesota

Blue Earth Books are published by Capstone Press
151 Good Counsel Drive, P.O. Box 669, Mankato, Minnesota 56002
http://www.capstone-press.com

Library of Congress Cataloging-in-Publication Data
Draper, Charla L.
  Cooking on nineteenth-century whaling ships / Charla Draper; consultant, Judy Downey.
    p. cm.—(Exploring history through simple recipes)
  ISBN 0-7368-0602-4
  1. Cookery, Marine—Juvenile literature. 2. Whaling ships—Juvenile literature. [1. Cookery, Marine. 2. Whaling ships.]
I. Title. II. Series.
TX840.M7 D73 2001
639.2'8'09730903—dc21
                                                    00-037958

Summary: Discusses everday life, duties, ports of call, foods, meals, cooking methods, and holidays of whaling ship crews in the early- to mid-1800s. Includes recipes and sidebars.

Editorial credits
Editors, Kay M. Olson, Kerry A. Graves; cover designer,
Steve Christensen; cover production and interior designer,
Heather Kindseth; illustrator, Linda Clavel; photo researcher,
Katy Kudela

Editor's note
Adult supervision may be needed for some recipes in this
book. All recipes have been tested. Although based on
historical foods, recipes have been modernized and simplified
for today's young cooks.

Photo credits
Mystic Seaport Museum, cover, 6–7, 8, 10, 12, 15 (all), 16 (left),
26; Gregg Andersen, cover background, 9, 16 (right), 23, 25
(top) 27; Scribner's Magazine (courtesy of Mystic Seaport
Museum), 11; San Francisco Maritime National Park, 13; New
York Public Library, 14; North Wind Picture Archives, 18, 19,
24, 28–29; Shelburne Museum, 20; Peabody Essex Museum,
25 (bottom)

1 2 3 4 5 6 06 05 04 03 02 01

Contents

Metric Conversion Guide

U.S.		Canada
¼ teaspoon		1 mL
½ teaspoon		2 mL
1 teaspoon		5 mL
1 tablespoon		15 mL
¼ cup		50 mL
⅓ cup		75 mL
½ cup		125 mL
⅔ cup		150 mL
¾ cup		175 mL
1 cup		250 mL
1 quart		1 liter
1 ounce		30 grams
2 ounces		55 grams
4 ounces		85 grams
½ pound		225 grams
1 pound		455 grams

Fahrenheit		Celsius
325 degrees		160 degrees
350 degrees		180 degrees
375 degrees		190 degrees
400 degrees		200 degrees
425 degrees		220 degrees

Kitchen Safety

1. Make sure your hair and clothes will not be in the way while you are cooking.

2. Keep a fire extinguisher in the kitchen. Never put water on a grease fire.

3. Wash your hands with soap before you start to cook. Wash your hands with soap again after you handle meat or poultry.

4. Ask an adult for help with sharp knives, the stove, the oven, and all electrical appliances.

5. Turn handles of pots and pans to the middle of the stove. A person walking by could run into handles that stick out toward the room.

6. Use dry pot holders to take dishes out of the oven.

7. Wash all fruits and vegetables.

8. Always use a clean cutting board. Wash the cutting board thoroughly after cutting meat or poultry.

9. Wipe up spills immediately.

10. Store leftovers properly. Do not leave leftovers out at room temperature for more than two hours.

4

Cooking Equipment

serving platter

liquid measuring cup

electric mixer

rolling pin

sharp knife

cutting board

serrated knife

Dutch oven

"instant read" thermometer

large and medium saucepans

colander

coffee can

stainless steel mixing bowl

measuring spoons

jar

mortar and pestle

can opener

vegetable peeler

tongs

trivet

wire whisk

mixing bowls

dry-ingredient measuring cups

slotted spoon

wooden spoon

spatula

rubber spatula

large skillet

fork

pot holder

COFFEE

Whaling's Golden Age

North Americans have hunted whales for thousands of years. Early American Indians used canoes to chase whales across shallow coastal waters. They cooked with whale blubber, ate whale meat, and carved whalebones into simple tools. In 1620, colonists arriving in America aboard the *Mayflower* noticed whales swimming near the ship. By 1640, colonists in New York had begun organized whaling along the eastern coast.

Whaling on the Atlantic Ocean quickly became a big business. As more immigrants came to North America, the demand for whale oil increased. Colonists used whale oil in products such as candles and soap. In the 1800s, Americans depended on whale oil for fuel to light lamps in their homes.

Whaling crews made oil from whale fat, called blubber. After killing a whale at sea, the crew cut the blubber away from a whale's body, stored it in casks, and brought the casks back to shore. At shore stations, the whalers then boiled the blubber in huge pots called trypots to release the valuable oil.

Whalers went farther out to sea seeking the huge animals. Longer voyages meant crews had to process whale blubber aboard large ships. These vessels were built for strength and were designed for sea voyages up to four years long.

The whaling industry reached its peak from the mid-1830s to the mid-1850s, a period known as the golden age of whaling. During this time, more than 700 American whaling ships took to the seas. Most of this fleet sailed from New Bedford, Massachusetts, known as "the whaling city." The New England coast had become the center of the U.S. whaling industry. During their most profitable years, whalers processed more than four million barrels of oil each year.

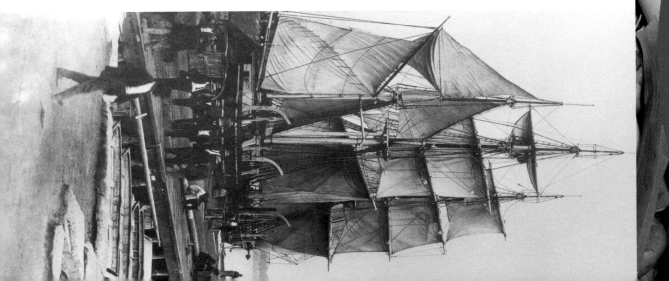

During the golden age, most whalers sailed in search of sperm whales, the most valuable of the hunted whales. Whalers could make 100 barrels of oil from the blubber of one large sperm whale. But whalers considered spermaceti the most valuable part of the sperm whale. This waxy substance is produced by the spermaceti organ in the whale's head. The head could hold about 25 gallons (95 liters) of spermaceti.

By the mid-1800s, whaling ship owners were making large profits from the sale of spermaceti. Companies used the substance to make lipstick, rouge, eye shadow, cold cream, and other cosmetics. A mixture of sperm whale oil and spermaceti was called sperm oil. Sperm oil was the main ingredient in high-quality candles used to light the homes of wealthy Americans.

Whaling began its decline at the end of the 1850s. In 1859, petroleum was discovered. Distilling merchants purified petroleum into kerosene, a fuel used for lanterns. Kerosene lanterns, which smoked and smelled as they burned, were not as convenient as clean-burning whale oil lanterns and candles. But by 1880, kerosene sold for 18 cents a gallon (4 liters) while the same amount of whale oil cost 51 cents. People were willing to put up with the smoke and smell of kerosene to save money.

Less demand for whale oil meant whaling ship profits declined. Ship owners had less money to make repairs and replace vessels lost at sea. In the early 1870s, fewer than 300 U.S. whaling ships were at sea. By 1872, the number had fallen to fewer than 200, and after 1890, there were fewer than 100 U.S. whaling ships. By the early 1900s, fewer than 50 whaling ships left from New England ports.

U.S. whaling continued into the 1900s, but whale oil profits were never again as high as during the golden age of whaling.

Stocking Up for the Voyage

Whaling ships stocked most of the supplies they needed for their voyage before they left their home port. Harpoons, rope, knives, oil barrels, and firewood filled storage areas below deck. The crew used these supplies for killing whales, cooking blubber, and storing oil. The ship also had to be stocked with enough food to feed hungry crew members for months at a time.

Food supplies on whaling ships often were dried or salted items. Raisins, dried beans, and salt pork did not spoil as quickly as fresh fruits, vegetables, and meat. Most whaling ships started their voyage with staple foods, including beans, peas, potatoes, turnips, corn, rice, sugar, flour, cornmeal, molasses, vinegar, and coffee. The ship's larder also might include tea, raisins, dried apples, salt pork, butter, and chocolate.

A storm at sea that followed a fresh pork meal was called "piggy's revenge."

Whaling ships carried livestock such as goats, pigs, chickens, and sheep on board. These animals provided the milk, butter, eggs, and fresh meat for the crew. The captain and the officers most often enjoyed fresh meat. But on occasion, a large hog was butchered and even the lowest ranking crew member ate fresh pork for dinner.

Fresh water was another important item that had to be stowed on board before the voyage. Crew members filled large casks, or barrels, with fresh water. The crew gathered rainwater during storms to refill the water casks. The crew also refilled the casks in port. But fresh water on land sometimes could only be found at a nearby muddy river. Whalers tried to make dirty water taste better by sweetening it with lemon syrup or boiling it and adding coffee or tea.

Cabbage and Irish Potatoes

Laws regulated the amount of basic supplies required on U.S. whaling ships. Provisions included some fresh foods, which the cook prepared early in the voyage before the food spoiled. One of the first meals whaling crew members had at the beginning of their voyage included cabbage and potatoes.

Ingredients

1 head cabbage, 2 to 3 pounds
  (1 to 1.5 kilograms)
white potatoes, 1 pound
  (.5 kilograms)
3 cups water
1 bay leaf
1 whole allspice
1 teaspoon salt

Equipment

cutting board
sharp knife
colander
vegetable peeler
Dutch oven or large saucepan with lid
liquid measuring cup
measuring spoons
cooking fork
slotted spoon

1. Cut cabbage head in half. Slice each half into three wedges. Trim away tough center core of each wedge. Rinse cabbage wedges in colander. Set aside.

2. Remove potato skins with vegetable peeler.

3. Cut each potato into four equal pieces.

4. In Dutch oven or large saucepan, combine 3 cups water, 1 bay leaf, 1 whole allspice, and 1 teaspoon salt. Bring ingredients to a boil. Reduce heat.

5. Use cooking fork to add cabbage wedges and potato pieces to boiling water. Dropping the cabbage wedges and potato pieces into the Dutch oven may cause boiling water to splash.

6. Reduce heat to low. Cover with lid.

7. Simmer vegetables 15 to 20 minutes until cabbage and potatoes are tender.

8. Remove cabbage wedges and potato pieces with a slotted spoon. Discard any remaining water, the bay leaf, and the whole allspice.

Makes 8 to 10 servings

Life at Sea

The ship's captain was responsible for everything aboard the whaling ship. His word was law. The captain navigated the ship's course, decided what ports to visit, provisions to bring on board, chose which provisions to bring on board, and kept discipline among the crew. The captain always had the aft, or rear, cabin on the starboard side of the ship. He also sat at the right side of the table at meals.

Whaling ships usually had two, three, or four officers on board. These officers, called mates, were next in line of authority after the captain. The first mate was the captain's first officer, the second mate was the captain's second officer, and on down the line. Besides helping the captain, the first mate kept the ship's official log. The first mate's duties included recording daily activities aboard the ship, encounters with whales, and the number of oil barrels produced from each kill.

Living quarters aboard a whaling ship were arranged according to rank. Mates had staterooms, which were smaller quarters than the captain's cabin. These staterooms were on the port side of the ship. The first mate's room was aft, the second mate's room was forward of the first mate's room, and so on.

Steerage rooms were situated between the mate's staterooms and the forecastle at the front of the ship. The steerage usually contained eight bunks, which were reserved for the boatsteerers, harpooners, and other skilled workers. The rest of the crew lived, slept, and ate

The men aboard whaling ships came from many backgrounds and often from other areas of the world. A ship's crew often included Native Americans, African Americans, Europeans, Azoreans, Cape Verdeans, West Indians, and South Sea Islanders.

Crew members lived, slept, and ate in the forecastle. The galley, or kitchen, usually was located here as well. Heat from the cookstove had the added benefit of warming the sailors during cold weather.

11

in the forecastle at the bow, or front, of the ship. This area usually had rough bunks and coarse tables.

In the mid-1800s, some captains brought their wives and children aboard to keep the family together during long voyages. Whaling ships with women and children aboard sometimes were called "lady ships." The captain's family shared in the better-quality food served on board, but whaling wives almost never cooked meals. The galley,

or kitchen, was located in the crew's sleeping quarters, which was off-limits to women and children.

Wives of whaling captains handled housekeeping duties in the family's living quarters. They sewed, did family laundry, cared for babies, and taught older children school lessons. The captain's wife sometimes taught willing whalers how to read. She often helped treat crew members' ailments and nursed sick men back to health.

The captain's cabin, or saloon, had the best of everything, including table, dishes, and food. The long, narrow strips along the table were called fiddles. These pieces of wood prevented the dishes from sliding off the table during rough sea weather. Tables for the crew also had fiddles but they were made of much rougher wood. Crew dishes usually were made of tin instead of china.

Roast Chicken

Ingredients
2 tablespoons dried parsley, crumbled
1 teaspoon dried thyme, crumbled
¾ teaspoon salt
¼ teaspoon pepper
cut-up fryer chicken, 2½ to 3 pounds
    (1 to 1.5 kilogram)

Equipment
measuring spoons
small bowl
wooden spoon
1-quart (1-liter) resealable plastic bag
tongs
large cast-iron skillet or oven-safe
    baking dish
pot holders
fork
instant-read thermometer

1. Preheat oven to 500°F (260°C).

2. Combine 2 tablespoons parsley, 1 teaspoon thyme, ¾ teaspoon salt, and ¼ teaspoon pepper. In a small bowl, blend seasoning mixture with a wooden spoon.

3. Place half of cut-up chicken in resealable plastic bag. Add half of seasoning mixture. Seal bag, shake to coat chicken pieces. Use tongs to remove chicken pieces and put them in cast-iron skillet or oven-safe baking dish skin-side up.

4. Repeat step 3 with remaining chicken and seasoning mixture.

5. Place chicken in preheated oven. Bake 10 minutes.

6. Reduce oven temperature to 350°F. Bake chicken 45 to 50 minutes until chicken is tender and soft when pierced with a fork. Chicken should cook to an inside temperature of 170°F (77°C). Take temperature reading by poking the pointed end of an instant-read thermometer into the thickest part of the chicken breast or thigh.

Makes 4 to 6 servings

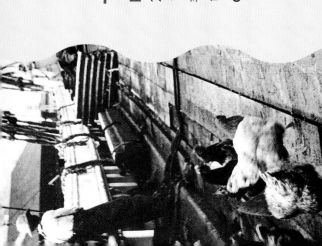

Chickens often were among the livestock carried aboard whaling ships. An unlucky chicken that stopped laying eggs often was butchered for the captain's Sunday meal.

Grub on Board

Meals on board whaling ships often were very different from home cooking. The ship's galley was crowded in with the crew's living quarters. There, the stove did double duty, heating the crew's sleeping area and cooking their food. Often the cook was a former whaler who had lost a hand or a foot in a shipboard accident and needed an easier job. If the ship's cook became sick, he almost always was replaced by the youngest forecastle apprentice or the clumsiest greenhand on deck.

The cook's main duty was to prepare food, keep the galley clean, and polish the cooking equipment, called coppers. All the cook really had to know about cooking was how to boil water. The cook routinely cut off a ration of salt beef or pork and soaked it for a while in seawater to remove the brine crust. He then would boil it in a big pot with some dried beans, peas, or other vegetables. Ship cooks also made sea biscuit, or hardtack. This hard cracker, which was made from flour, salt, and water, did not break or spoil like regular crackers.

The barrels, boxes, and crates of food on board attracted bugs, worms, and rats. These pests found their way onto the ship at every port. The food quickly spoiled. Cornmeal and flour usually were infested with weevils. Maggots floated to the top of pea soup. Whalers called rice the "happy hunting ground" as they picked out small, black bugs. Worms crawled into the holes in sea biscuits and stayed there.

The Galapagos Islands in the Pacific were known as the Tortoise Islands. Whalers captured giant sea turtles and feasted on the fresh meat.

The cook's menu rarely varied, and the crew often could tell the day of the week by the food on their plates. Cooks prepared and served meals according to rank. The captain and ship's officers ate the best quality and variety of food. They enjoyed delicacies such as butter and sugar. Skilled crewmen, including boatsteerers and harpooners, used molasses to sweeten their coffee and tea. But regular crew members drank these beverages black. The crew's coffee and tea were so thick and strong that they seldom could see the bottom of the cup.

Some food specialties were found on board almost any whaling ship, no matter who the cook might be. Sea pies were a flour dumpling that contained meat and the ground bones of porpoises. Lobscouse was a type of stew made from salted meat, onions, pepper, and sea biscuits. Duff, a type of fruitcake, was a regular shipboard menu item made from lard, flour, molasses, and yeast.

The ship's cook followed the mess bill and repeated menu items each week. At the end of a voyage, captains sold any leftover cooking grease. The cook got a percentage of profits from this grease, called slush. Some cooks purposely skimped on grease in their cooking so they would have a bigger slush fund.

Occasionally, when crew members had time to catch a fish or two, the cook might serve fresh fish for dinner. But whalers had to be careful because some species were poisonous. Cooks had to take extra care with fish caught in port. Copper salts leaked into harbor waters from the hulls of some sailing ships. The cook tested the fish for poison by cooking it with a silver coin. If the coin turned black, the cook had to throw away the fish.

The cook prepared meals for the captain and crew in the galley of the ship. This galley is more modern than typical ship galleys in whaling ships of the 1800s.

Lobscous

Ingredients

3/4 pound corned beef
3/4 pound smoked ham
2 medium onions
3 medium potatoes
2 medium leeks
3 tablespoons bacon grease or vegetable oil
1/2 cup water
1/2 cup cracker meal
3 juniper berries*
1/2 teaspoon allspice
1/2 teaspoon nutmeg
1/2 teaspoon mace
1/2 teaspoon ground cloves
1/2 teaspoon ground cardamom
1/4 teaspoon salt (optional)
1/8 teaspoon pepper (optional)

*Look for juniper berries at stores that sell bulk spices.

Equipment

cutting board
sharp knife
vegetable peeler
2 medium-sized bowls
measuring spoons
large skillet
wooden spoon
large slotted spoon
empty coffee can or container
colander
dry-ingredient measuring cups
liquid measuring cup
rolling pin or mortar and pestle

1. Cut corned beef and smoked ham into ¼-inch (.6-centimeter) cubes. Set aside.

2. Peel and slice onions. Cut slices into ¼-inch (.10-centimeter) cubes. Set aside.

3. Remove skin from potatoes with vegetable peeler. Cut potatoes into ¼-inch (.10-centimeter) cubes. Put potato cubes in medium-sized bowl and add enough water to cover them. This step keeps potatoes from turning dark. Set aside.

4. Trim roots and tough green stem from leek. Cut remaining leek in half lengthwise. Wash leek under running water while separating layers to remove grit. Cut leeks into ¼-inch (.10-centimeter) slices. Set aside.

5. In large skillet, heat 3 tablespoons bacon grease or vegetable oil. Add cubed corned beef and cubed ham. Cook 10 to 15 minutes on medium heat. Stir.

6. With slotted spoon, remove meat from skillet and put in medium-sized bowl. Pour fat into an empty coffee can or other container. Measure 3 tablespoons of these

7. drippings and add them to skillet.

8. Add onions to skillet. Cook over medium heat for 5 to 6 minutes or until onions are soft.

9. Add leeks to onions in skillet. Cook over medium heat until onions are clear and start to brown.

10. Pour potatoes and water through colander to drain. Add potatoes to skillet. Cook over medium heat for 5 minutes, stirring often.

11. Return the cooked corned beef and smoked ham to the skillet. Cover and cook over medium heat for 8 to 10 minutes, or until fork can easily pierce potatoes.

12. Add ½ cup cracker meal and ½ cup water to ingredients in skillet. If you prefer a moist, saucy lobscouse, add ¼ cup to ½ cup more water. Mix until blended.

13. With rolling pin or mortar and pestle, crush three juniper berries.

14. Add 3 crushed juniper berries, ½ teaspoon allspice, ½ teaspoon nutmeg, ½ teaspoon mace, ½ teaspoon ground cloves, and ½ teaspoon cardamom. If desired, add ¼ teaspoon salt and ⅛ teaspoon pepper. Mix until blended.

15. Cover and cook 5 minutes over low heat.

Makes 4 to 5 servings

Making Whale Oil

After making the kill, the crew towed the whale carcass back to the ship and began the process of making whale oil. They tied the dead whale alongside the ship. Some of the crew members balanced on a wooden platform suspended above the dead whale. There they cut the whale's blubber with long-handled spades or knives. The crew removed the blubber in long strips called blanket pieces. Each strip weighed about 1 ton (1 metric ton). Crew members hauled the blanket pieces onto the ship's deck with a giant hook attached to a rope and pulley.

Crew members on deck prepared the blubber for boiling. They cut the blanket pieces into smaller strips called horse pieces. They then cut the horse pieces into thinner slices. At this point, the whale's skin looked like a book binding and the blubber looked like thick book pages. Whalers called these pieces Bible leaves.

Bible leaves were the right size to try out in a large pot. Crew members started a fire in the brick furnace of the tryworks. Huge trypots held the cooking blubber. The heat shriveled the blubber, and oil slowly rose to the top of the pot. Each trypot could hold 300 to 400 gallons (1,100 to 1,500 liters) of whale oil. After the blubber cooked away, crew members ladled the hot oil from the trypot into a cooling tank. Workers

Crew members hauled blanket pieces of whale blubber on deck. They cut the blubber into strips called horse pieces. Smaller, thinner slices were called Bible leaves. These pieces were the right size to boil, or try out.

Hunting the Whale

The crew chased and killed whales. The captain divided the crew into watches to look for whales. Watches lasted four hours, except for two two-hour late-afternoon "dog watches." A bell sounded each half hour of a watch. One bell marked the first half hour, and two bells marked the second half hour. The end of a watch was marked with eight bells.

During each watch, crew members took turns being the lookout. A lookout stood atop the masthead, which was 100 feet (30 meters) above the ship's deck. The lookout watched for a huge spout of misting water. When the lookout spied a whale spout, he cried, "There she blows."

When a whale was spotted, the crew ran to stations on the deck. A ship had three to five whaleboats hanging over the side on davit poles. The crew climbed into the whaleboats, lowered the boats into the water, and rowed to chase the whale.

Whalers had to be quick and strong. A crew of six men rowed each small whaleboat, which was about 30 feet (9 meters) long and 6 feet (2 meters) wide. The harpooner stood at the front of the whaleboat and aimed a 10-foot-long (3-meter-long) harpoon at a spot just behind the whale's head.

Harpooned whales put up a mighty struggle. They tried to escape the whalers by thrashing, rolling, and sounding in the water. When a whale sounds, it dives deep into the ocean. The harpoon used to spear the whale was attached to rope about 1,800 feet (550 meters) long. The wounded whale sometimes swam for hours, pulling along the whaleboat and crew. The whale eventually tired and floated to the ocean's surface. The boatsteerer then made the final kill with a razor-sharp lance.

Clouds of black smoke rose from the whaling ship while the crew cooked whale blubber into oil. They boiled the blubber in huge trypots over a brick furnace called a tryworks.

poured the cooked oil into large barrels. They stowed the oil barrels in the ship's hold below deck.

Other valuable parts of the whale also were processed on board the ship. Workers removed the spermaceti from the whale's head. They quickly scalded the spermaceti in a trypot and then poured it into storage barrels. Crewmen probed the whale's intestines with long spades. They sometimes found a rare substance called ambergris, formed of undigested food. Whaling ship owners sold this waxy substance to manufacturers who used it to make perfume.

Chasing, killing, and trying out a whale took about two to three days. The crew worked throughout the day and night in six-hour shifts. They usually did not take time to eat a meal together. When the crew had made 1,000 barrels of oil, the cook marked the occasion by making doughnuts. He brought the batter on deck and fried the doughnuts in whale oil.

Whalers still had to eat some food during the whale processing, even though they did not sit together at meal time. During the trying out time, a cook might leave a kettle of salt pork and beans simmering for crew members to eat after their shift. Other times, the hungry men dipped sea biscuits into salt water and fried them in whale oil. Workers might chop a little whale meat with potatoes to fry into a fritter. While the whale oil was cooking, crisp bits of blubber floated to the top of the pot. Crew members ate these crispy cracklings as a quick snack.

Salt Pork and Beans

This recipe must be started the night before serving.

Ingredients

1⅓ cups Great Northern beans or
    navy beans
5 cups water
1 tablespoon lard or shortening
1 medium onion
1½ quarts (1.4 liters) water
⅓ pound (.15 kilogram) salt pork
5 red pepper flakes or 1 black peppercorn

Equipment

dry-ingredient measuring cups
4-quart (3.8-liter) Dutch oven or
    large saucepan with lid
colander
cutting board
sharp knife
measuring spoons
liquid measuring cup
wooden spoon
pot holders

1. Put beans in Dutch oven or saucepan. Cover beans with water and soak overnight.
2. The next day, pour beans and water into colander to drain water. Set aside.
3. Dry the inside of the Dutch oven or large saucepan.
4. With the knife, peel and thinly slice onions. Chop slices into small pieces.
5. Add 1 tablespoon lard to Dutch oven or saucepan. Cook on low until lard melts.
6. Add chopped onions. Cook on medium heat, stirring until onions are starting to brown. Using pot holders, remove Dutch oven or large saucepan from heat.
7. Add 1½ quarts (1.4 liters) water, ⅓ pound (10 grams) salt pork, and drained beans, and 5 red pepper flakes to Dutch oven or saucepan.
8. Using pot holders, return Dutch oven or saucepan to heat. Bring mixture to a boil, stirring several times.
9. Reduce heat to low. Cover. Let mixture simmer 1 to 2 hours, stirring often to prevent beans from sticking. Use pot holders to remove Dutch oven or saucepan from heat.

Makes 6 to 8 servings

"Our fare since we have been at sea has been nothing but salt cod, pork and hard bread. The pork [is] at least five years old, the water is very bad."

—Thomas Rose,
Chelsea, 1831

W halers who sailed in the Atlantic Ocean in the mid-1800s usually left from ports near New Bedford, Massachusetts, in the spring. They sailed east toward the Azores, a group of islands in the mid-Atlantic. The Azores were an early port of call for Atlantic whaling ships. The crew could pick up supplies on these islands. By the time ships reached the Azores, the crew's store of fresh food had begun to run out. The warm, temperate climate in this area of the world offered plenty of fresh fruit and vegetables, as well as fresh water.

From the Azores, the ships traveled south along the western coast of Africa. Whaling ships then turned west toward the coast of Brazil in South America. Whaling ships returned to their home port around the end of spring. With fresh supplies, the ship then headed north to Davis Straits near Greenland for the summer.

The ports of call were important to the crew for many reasons. Some men became whalers for the opportunity to see the world. Ports of call gave them the chance to see cities in other countries. Going ashore for a short time also helped ease the boredom of many months at sea.

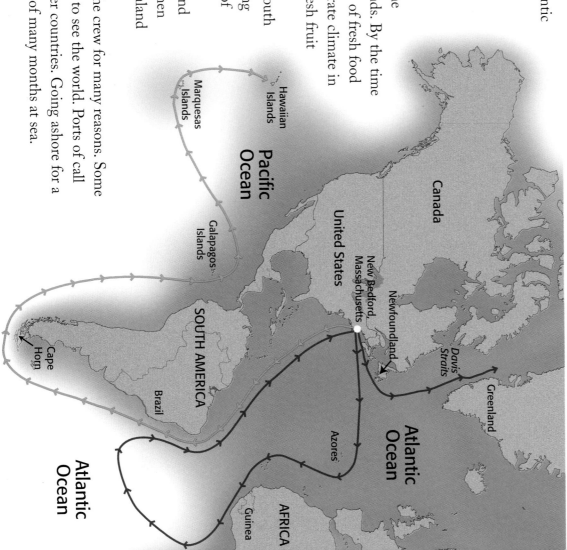

Pacific Ocean

Hawaiian Islands

Marquesas Islands

Galapagos Islands

Canada

United States

New Bedford, Massachusetts

Newfoundland

Davis Straits

Greenland

Atlantic Ocean

SOUTH AMERICA

Brazil

Cape Horn

Azores

Guinea

AFRICA

Atlantic Ocean

Pumpkin Soup

Ingredients

- 1 small onion
- 2 tablespoons butter
- 2 tablespoons flour
- 1 cup milk
- 1 15-ounce can of 100% pure pumpkin
- 1⅓ cups water
- 2 tablespoons brown sugar
- ¼ teaspoon salt
- ¼ teaspoon allspice
- 6 tablespoons sour cream*
- 3 teaspoons brown sugar*

optional ingredients

Equipment

- cutting board
- sharp knife
- large saucepan
- measuring spoons
- wooden spoon or wire whisk
- can opener
- rubber spatula or large spoon
- liquid measuring cup

1. Peel outer layer of onion. Cut in half. Chop one half into small pieces. Set other half aside.

2. In saucepan, melt 2 tablespoons butter on low heat.

3. Add 2 tablespoons chopped onions to melted butter in saucepan. Cook on low heat, stirring until onions begin to brown.

4. Add 2 tablespoons flour. Stir with spoon or whisk until blended.

5. Slowly pour in 1 cup milk, stirring constantly. Cook on low until mixture is smooth and thick. Remove from heat.

6. Open can of pumpkin. With spatula or spoon, remove half of the pumpkin and put in saucepan. Pour 1⅓ cups water into saucepan. Heat and stir until blended.

7. Add remaining half can of pumpkin. Stir until blended.

8. Continue cooking over medium heat, stirring occasionally, until mixture is hot and steam is visible when a spoonful of soup is lifted from the pan.

9. Add 2 tablespoons brown sugar, ¼ teaspoon salt, and ¼ teaspoon allspice. Stir until blended.

10. Garnish each serving with 1 tablespoon dairy sour cream and ½ teaspoon brown sugar, if desired.

Makes 6 servings

Main Whaling Routes of the mid-1800s

— Atlantic route

⁃ ⁃ ⁃ Pacific route

Whaling on the Pacific

By the 1840s, the U.S. whaling industry included more than 700 ships. Many of these ships sailed the Pacific Ocean's whaling grounds. A popular route started in New England and went south along the coast of South America. Ships traveled around the tip of the continent, and then sailed north to the coast of Central America. From there, the captain charted a westward course.

Ports in the Pacific included the Galapagos, the Marquesas, and the Hawaiian Islands. The weather in these ports was sunny and warm. Whalers had plenty of fresh food such as breadfruit, bananas, plantains, coconuts, oranges, pineapples, papayas, and figs. The crew also replenished supplies of livestock with chickens and pigs at these tropical ports of call.

The Hawaiian Islands were a popular port for whaling ships in the Pacific Ocean. The crew went ashore while the ship was docked for repairs.

By the time a whaling crew reached Honolulu, Hawaii, the ship often needed major repairs. While the ship was docked, the crew, captain, and any of his family members on board enjoyed extended shore visits. The captain saw to the ship repairs and hired merchant ships to take the whale oil back to New England. This arrangement created space for the new barrels of whale oil that the captain hoped to process during the rest of the voyage.

During the golden age of whaling, many New Englanders visited with hometown friends at these ports. Some families had temporary homes on the islands while their husbands and fathers returned to sea and the whaling grounds near Japan and in the Arctic.

Pacific Fruit Plate

Ingredients	Equipment
1 fresh pineapple	cutting board
3 oranges	lightweight kitchen towel
3 bananas	knife
¼ cup shredded coconut	dry-ingredient measuring cups
	serving platter or plate
	spoon

Families and crew members aboard whaling ships visited each other while at sea. These visits, called gams, gave everyone aboard the chance to share news, trade supplies, and have some fun.

1. Wrap a towel around the green leaves of the pineapple crown. Twist crown to remove it.

2. Place pineapple on cutting board and cut in half lengthwise.

3. Cut both pineapple pieces in half lengthwise.

4. Place each quarter cut-side down on cutting board. With knife, cut core that runs the length of fruit from each quarter. Discard core pieces. Cut each quarter pineapple crosswise into 1-inch (2.5-centimeter) slices. Arrange on platter.

5. Cut oranges in half. Cut each half into six wedge-shaped pieces. Arrange on plate.

6. Peel bananas and cut each banana into 1-inch (2.5-centimeter) slices. Arrange on plate.

8. Sprinkle ¼ cup shredded coconut evenly over fruit.

Makes 4 to 6 servings

When whaling voyages lasted a year or more, the crew celebrated special days on board. Fourth of July and Christmas both were popular holidays for New Englanders. The ship's captain determined how much celebrating would be allowed. Stingy captains might make their crews work the same number of hours on holidays as they did other days of the year. More generous captains might allow the crew a day of rest and order special foods to be served for the holiday meals.

A whaling ship's holiday menu might include traditional dishes such as chicken or pork. Choice meats usually were reserved for the captain's table. The crew may have been served a bite or two of meat, but it often was cooked in soup or stew. Sweet breads, puddings, or mincemeat pie were served for dessert. The traditional holiday dessert for whalers was duff, a kind of boiled pudding similar to fruitcake.

The cook usually served duff for Christmas. This boiled pudding was a favorite of the ship's crew.

Holiday Duff

Ingredients

2 quarts (2 liters) water
2 tablespoons solid
  shortening for greasing
½ cup packed brown sugar
¼ cup shortening
1 egg
¼ cup molasses
½ cup milk
½ cup cracker meal
1 cup raisins
¾ cup flour

1 teaspoon baking powder
½ teaspoon cinnamon
¼ teaspoon each of: baking
  soda, ginger, nutmeg,
  ground cloves
½ cup powdered sugar

Equipment

8-quart (7.5-liter) stockpot or
  Dutch oven with lid
paper towel
medium stainless steel bowl
medium mixing bowl
1 stainless steel trivet
large mixing bowl
dry-ingredient measuring
  cups
electric mixer
small mixing bowl
measuring spoons
wooden spoon
liquid measuring cup
aluminum foil
fork

pot holders
metal spatula or knife
serving plate
serrated knife

1. Place trivet inside the stockpot or Dutch oven. Add 2 quarts (2 liters) water. Cover and cook over low heat.

2. With paper towel and 2 tablespoons shortening, lightly grease inside of the medium stainless steel bowl.

3. In large mixing bowl, combine ½ cup brown sugar and ⅓ cup shortening. With electric mixer, blend well.

4. Using a fork, beat the egg in a small mixing bowl until the yolk is completely mixed with the egg white.

5. Add the beaten egg, ¼ cup molasses, ½ cup milk, ½ cup cracker meal, and 1 cup raisins to sugar and shortening mixture. Blend well with electric mixer.

6. In medium mixing bowl, add ¾ cup flour, 1 teaspoon baking powder, ½ teaspoon cinnamon, and ¼ teaspoon each baking soda, ginger, nutmeg, and cloves. Mix well.

7. Add combined flour mixture to molasses mixture. With electric mixer, mix until well-blended.

8. Pour batter into the greased stainless steel bowl. Cover tightly with aluminum foil. Place bowl in stockpot or Dutch oven. Cover.

9. Cook on high until steam begins to escape. Reduce heat to low. Continue cooking for 1½ hours. Add more water to keep the Dutch oven from becoming dry.

10. Turn off burner. Using pot holders remove bowl. Prick foil with fork. Wait 10 minutes before removing foil.

11. Loosen duff from bowl with a metal spatula or knife. Cover bowl with serving plate. Turn over plate and slightly shake bowl to make duff fall onto plate.

12. Sprinkle each serving with powdered sugar, if desired.

Makes 8 to 10 servings

Homeward Bound

At the end of a successful whaling voyage, the ship's cargo hold was full of whale oil. Returning ships had barrels stacked tightly in the hold. Most whaling ships also brought home whalebone and bundles of baleen, a lightweight, flexible material found in the mouths of certain whales. Some whalers brought along foods from tropical ports of call.

On their long ocean voyage, crew members ate the same quality and quantity of food day after day. Once home, whalers were eager for some New England home cooking. They looked forward to tasting favorite foods and dishes such as boiled ham, cabbage, succotash, baked beans, Indian pudding, fresh bread, butter, cakes, and pies.

The most traditional New England meal was chowder. During the 1800s, the word chowder in New England meant both a social event and a meal. The main ingredients in a traditional chowder meal are fresh fish, salt pork, hard bread or biscuits, and water. Whalers often had the ingredients for chowder on board during the voyage. But the rich taste of this special dish tasted best at home.

After a voyage, the ship returned to its home port. Here an old whaling ship is hove down for repairs near New Bedford, Massachusetts, known as the whaling city.

New England Clam Chowder

Ingredients

small onion
1/4 pound (1 kilogram) salt pork*
2 medium potatoes
1 1/2 cups water
1 6 1/2-ounce can minced clams in juice
1 8-ounce bottle of clam juice
1/8 teaspoon pepper
1 1/2 cups milk

Equipment

medium saucepan with lid
wooden spoon
cutting board
sharp knife
slotted spoon
vegetable peeler
cooking fork
can opener
liquid measuring cup

*Look for salt pork in the grocery meat department with fresh pork or smoked meats.

1. Cut 1/4 pound (1 kilogram) salt pork into 1-inch (2.5-centimeter) pieces.
2. Peel and chop onion into 1/4-inch (.10-centimeter) pieces. Set aside.
3. In saucepan, cook salt pork pieces over medium heat. Turn pieces with spatula and cook 10 to 12 minutes, until salt pork browns.
4. Remove salt pork. Set aside.
5. With vegetable peeler, remove skin from potatoes. Slice potatoes 1/8 inch (.3 centimeters) thick. Set aside.
6. Add chopped onion to saucepan. Cook over medium heat, stirring occasionally.
7. Add potato slices to saucepan. Cover with 1 1/2 cups water. Cover and cook over low heat 10 to 12 minutes until potatoes are very tender.
8. Add can of clams (do not drain), 8-ounce bottle of clam juice, and 1/8 teaspoon pepper.
9. Cook over medium heat until steamy.
10. Add 1 1/2 cups milk. Heat 5 minutes over medium heat.

Makes 6 servings

Words to Know

aft (AFT)—toward the stern, or rear, of a ship

ambergris (AM-bahr-gris)—a waxy substance from the intestines of a sperm whale

Azores (AY-Zzorz)—a group of nine islands in the mid-Atlantic that belonged to Portugal

baleen (bah-LEEN)—rows of long, thin bone; baleen whales have baleen instead of teeth.

blubber (BLUH-bur)—the fat under the skin of a whale

brine (BRINE)—salty water used to preserve foods

carcass (KAR-kuhss)—the body of a dead animal

coppers (KOP-urs)—pots and pans in a ship's galley

deck (DEK)—the floor of a ship

forecastle (FOH-kah-sel)—the crew's quarters in the forward part of a ship

galley (GAL-ee)—the kitchen on a ship

larder (LAR-dur)—a small room or pantry in which food is stored

spermaceti (SPURM-uh-see-tee)—a substance found in the head of sperm whales that was used to make candles, lotions, and other goods

starboard (STAR-bord)—the right side of a ship

stern (STERN)—the back end of a ship

To Learn More

Baldwin, Robert F. *New England Whaler.* Minneapolis: Lerner Publications, 1996.

Chrisp, Peter. *The Whalers.* The Remarkable World. New York: Thomson Learning, 1995.

Jernegan, Laura. *A Whaling Captain's Daughter: The Diary of Laura Jernegan, 1868–1871,* edited by Megan O'Hara. Mankato, Minn.: Blue Earth Books, 2000.

McKissack, Patrica C. and Frederick L. *Black Hands, White Sails: The Story of African-American Whalers.* New York: Scholastic Press, 1999.

Murphy, Jim. *Gone A-Whaling: The Lure of the Sea and the Hunt for the Great Whale.* New York: Clarion Books, 1998.

Solheim, James. *It's Disgusting — and We Ate It!: Wild and wacky food from around the world—and throughout history!* New York: Simon & Schuster Books for Young Readers, 1998.

Places to Write and Visit

Kendall Whaling Museum
P.O. Box 297
27 Everett Street
Sharon, MA 02067

Mystic Seaport
P.O. Box 6000
75 Greenmanville Avenue
Mystic, CT 06355-0990

New Bedford Whaling Museum
18 Johnny Cake Hill
New Bedford, MA 02740-6398

Vancouver Maritime Museum
Vanier Park
905 Ogden Avenue
Vancouver, BC V6J 1A3
Canada

Whalers Village Museum
2435 Kaanapali Parkway
#H-16
Lahaina, HI 96761

Internet Sites

All About Whales!
http://www.EnchantedLearning.com/subjects/whales

Discovering Whales
http://whales.magna.com.au/DISCOVER/

Mystic Seaport
http://www.mystic.org

New Bedford Whaling Museum
http://www.whalingmuseum.org

The Kendall Whaling Museum
http://www.kwm.org

Index